THE BEASTLY GAZETTE

BUD & LOLO DELANEY, eds.

CARTOONS BY TOM EATON

SCHOLASTIC BOOK SERVICES
New York Toronto London Auckland Sydney Tokyo

Text copyright © 1977 by Francis Delaney, Jr. and Lolo Delaney. Illustrations copyright © 1977 by Scholastic Magazines, Inc. All rights reserved. Published by Scholastic Book Services, a division of Scholastic Magazines, Inc.

12 11 10 9 8 7 6 5 4 3 2 1   3   7 8 9/7 0 1 2/8

Printed in the U.S.A.   01

CONTENTS

1.

Raining Cats and Dogs

COLLEGE GIVES DOG A 'SPECIAL DEGREE'

SAN DIEGO, Calif. (AP) — Because she knows her way around, Gretchen was awarded a special degree by the University of San Diego Law School.

Her diploma was smaller than the other 173 conferred at the ceremonies, but that doesn't mean she didn't work as hard as anyone else.

It is just that Gretchen is a Doberman pinscher guide dog who did such a good job for her master, 40-year-old Robert D. Deens, that it was decided she deserved a PHT degree.

The letters stand for "putting him through," a variation of the "putting hubby through" mock degree sometimes given to wives of graduates.

"She certainly deserves it," Mr. Deens said. "She has seen me through four years at San Diego State and three years at U.S.D."

Mr. Deens, blinded by glaucoma, is a widower, who said he planned to be a general practice lawyer.

Thieves Steal Watchdog

PLAINFIELD, N.J. (AP) — The police report a burglar kicked in the rear door of Mrs. Wilma Barnett's home here and stole a television set, the kitchen clock and Mrs. Barnett's full-grown German shepherd watchdog.

Radio Soothes Dogs in Kennel

WICKHAMFORD, England (UPI) — The National Canine Defense League's home for stray dogs at Wickhamford has put a radio in each of its kennels. Superintendent Alan Barnard, 43, says his 60 dogs have just about stopped barking now that he keeps the radios turned on from dawn to dusk.

"I got the idea when I heard that cows were soothed by music," Bernard said. "But we found that dogs definitely prefer talk programs to music. They must find the human voice reassuring."

Family Dog in Ohio Enjoys Going to Classes in School

AKRON, Ohio (AP) — Duke has been in the second grade at Betty Jane School about six years. But no one is worried. He's a dog.

The 7-year-old beagle first went to the school when his owners, the George Adolphsons, had their oldest son there. They now have two sons attending the school.

"He loves school whether the kids go or not," Mrs. Adolphson said. "If the children are sick I say, 'Duke, they're not going to school today.' And Duke is off."

Simple Device Rescues Dog

LONDON (AP) — Heavy earthmoving equipment failed to reach a terrier trapped four days in a 30-foot crevice. Then the dog's owner dangled his cap at the end of a rope into the hole. The terrier sank his teeth into the cap and was hauled to the surface.

Hard-Working Agent Has No Time for Talk

SAN YSIDRO, Calif. (UPI)—His bosses listened to the speech. Link stayed on the job.

Link is one of the German shepherds that customs agents use at this border crossing point to sniff out marijuana in cars coming from Mexico.

Thursday, the border station was the scene of a ceremony. Vernon D. Acree, U.S. commissioner of customs, was dedicating 14 new gates. As he gave his speech, Link, sitting in the ranks, growled.

The commissioner continued. Link's hackles rose. A louder growl. "Shut up, Link," a handler hissed.

Link growled again. He bounded out of ranks and ran to a sedan waiting to pass through the new gates. Agents found a package of marijuana hidden behind the car's headlight and another in the gas tank.

Poodle on Coast
Gets Prescription for
Lenses

BERKELEY, Calif. (UPI) — Mr. Charley, a gray poodle, has good vision, but only when he is wearing his prescription glasses.

His owner, Harold Holdnash, said he had provided the spectacles so that Mr. Charley could watch the entertainment with him at local bistros without squinting.

Pet Dog Likes to Ride
On Top of Master's Car

BISHOPVILLE, S. C. (AP) — Coke Scarborough has a pet dog named Teddy who loves to go auto riding—while resting on the top of the car.

Teddy, as sure-footed as a mountain lion, sits up on the car top when the driver goes up to 50 or 60 miles an hour.

A Japanese Restaurant Caters to Canine Guests

TOKYO (AP) — A plush new restaurant in downtown Tokyo caters exclusively to chaperoned canine guests.

Called "Dog Beauty," the restaurant serves breakfast, lunch, dinner and special courses either on tables or on the establishment's carpeted floor.

Prices range from 40 cents to $1.40 a meal.

DOG GONE

NEW YORK (UPI) — From the strange claim file of an insurance company: Left unattended in the front seat of a car with motor running a pooch opted for reverse, hitting the gear shift lever. The auto rammed into a neighbor's garage across the street. The insurance company paid for the damage.

DOG IN ARIZONA GETS CROWN IN ITS TOOTH

GLENDALE, Ariz. (AP)—"PV," a dog owned by Judy Messer, sports a gold crown in her mouth.

When PV broke her left canine tooth recently, Miss Messer, co-owner of a crown and bridge dental laboratory here, decided to make a crown for the tooth. She came up with a gold one decorated with a dollar sign and inlaid with white dental acrylic.

"There's a practical reason for the crown being gold," Miss Messer explained, "It's actually a dental gold, alloyed with platinum and paladium. It's about the strongest substance used by dentists right now. We don't really know what will withstand a dog chewing on a bone."

The crown was installed by a dentist with the help of a veterinarian.

Dog Mistakes Policeman For Prowler, Falls 120 Feet

ATHERTON, Calif. Jan. 2 (UPI)—A police dog who mistook an officer for a prowler and plunged 120 feet from a rooftop is expected to be released from an animal hospital in a day or two.

"He's pretty sore now," Atherton Police Chief Greg Smith said of the dog, named Nando. "But I took him out for a walk and he wanted to get in the car and go to work."

Nando was chasing a scent on Sunday when a policeman jumped onto the roof from a Fire Department ladder.

The dog mistook the officer's scent for that of the burglar and ran across the roof and off the edge.

The dog's fall was broken by an overhang 60 feet down. His injuries consisted of a broken jaw and three broken teeth.

The suspected prowler was not caught.

Dog Returns
With 'Company'

DAYTON, Ohio (AP) — Harry Bean not only got back what he lost but more than he bargained for. When his missing Great Dane, Dixie, was traced to a farm wagon about 1½ miles from his house, she had given birth to 10 puppies.

Dog's Haircut
Brings Suit

SEATTLE (UPI)—Audrey Grandy sued a veterinarian for $5,000 damages, arguing that her sheepdog was sheared when all she wanted was to have the animal X-rayed.

German Shepherd in Lake Is Almost 'Caught' by Fish

SUDBURY, England (UPI)— Barney, a 98-pound German shepherd, was having his daily paddle in a lake when a huge pike clamped its jaw on his leg and almost pulled him under.

Barney's master, Tony Wright, said he hauled the three-year-old dog to safety with the 15-pound pike still clamped on Barney's leg.

The pike then let go and flopped back into the water.

"A smaller dog would have drowned," Mr. Wright said.

Dog Rescued After Leap From Bridge

REDWOOD CITY, Calif. (AP)—Daniel Brown's dog decided to go for a swim but he chose a rather unorthodox way to do it.

Brown, of Castro Valley, was eastbound on the San Mateo Bridge when the dog jumped out of his pickup truck and fell 30 feet over the rail into the San Francisco Bay.

Homer Ellett, a tow truck driver who regularly patrols the bridge in search of stranded motorists, saw the dog's dive and set out to rescue the floundering animal.

Ellett was lowered over the side on the tow truck's cable and was within inches of the dog when Brown yelled from the bridge above, "Hey, I forgot to tell you, the dog is vicious."

Ellett said the dog was too tired to resist and the rescue was successful.

'Careless' Kansan Eats What Dog Leaves Over

BENNINGTON, Kan. (AP) —Dick Belden, who lives on a farm near here, took three prime T-bone steaks from his freezer and put them on a table to thaw while he went out-of-doors to chop some wood.

In the meantime, Mr. Belden's dog smelled the meat, forced open the back door and proceeded to consume the steaks.

The Beldens had hamburgers for supper.

FAMILY DOG REVIVED BY HEART MASSAGE

HARTFORD, Sept. 11 (AP)—
"I would have left home rather than try to explain a dead dog to my daughter," said Lee Prettyman of Hartford after he revived the family dog from an electric shock.

Mr. Prettyman, a sea diver and teacher of aquatic sports, said that his daughter's puppy, a shepherd-husky crossbreed, had chewed through a lamp cord in their bedroom.

When he awoke at 5 A.M., he said, he found the dog "stiff as a board, eyes open, mouth shut and heart stopped . . . from all apparent signs he was dead."

The diver began administering heart massage and, in a short time, "the mouth opened and he started breathing and the tongue came out," Mr. Prettyman said.

"Finally, the pup turned and he licked me in the face. It was the greatest thing in the world."

A GERMAN SHEPHERD RUNS SOME ERRANDS

HUNTINGTON, W. Va. (AP) —Anytime she forgets something at a corner grocery, Mrs. John Earls only needs to call the store, order what she needs, then say to the family dog, Nemo, "Go to the store."

Off goes the pedigreed German shepherd down the block.

A few minutes later, he's back, with a small package hanging from between his teeth.

"It started when he was about six months old," said Mrs. Earls. "He'd see me getting out of the car and he'd jump on me, wanting to hold my pocketbook. From there, we taught him how to hold onto little sacks. He caught on in two or three sessions."

COLLIE STOWS AWAY UNDER A MAIL PLANE

PORT NEVILLE, British Columbia (AP)—The collie owned by the postmaster of this coastal town probably had sore toenails recently, and if he could talk he would probably have a few low-flying stories to tell.

Postmaster Olaf Hansen said he saw his full-grown pet collie on the docks just as the bags of mail were being unloaded from the mail plane.

When he looked again he saw the plane lifting off the water for its next stop about 20 miles away —with his collie clinging to one of its pontoons.

Mr. Hansen said the dog disembarked at the next stop and returned home the next day—in the cabin of the plane.

Dog Wandering in California Has a License Dated 1928

HOLLYWOOD (UPI) — An Afghan dog found wandering the streets puzzled animal shelter officials when they examined his collar and found a city dog license for 1928-29.

Edward Sidell, 24 years old, solved the mystery when he reported that the animal was his and the brass-studded leather collar and license had been inherited from his grandmother.

Mr. Sidell, an antique collector, said the collar originally was worn by his grandmother's dog, which was run over by a Model T Ford in 1929.

DOG IN AN ELEVATOR CAUSES STIR IN PARIS

PARIS (AP) — A dog got trapped in an elevator at Orly Airport. He growled, so no one got in. The door closed too fast for him to get out, and people who called for help didn't ease the confusion.

One person called the dog pound, but got the auto pound instead, and a man with a tow truck showed up.

In the next call the term "angry boxer" was taken to mean a berserk pugilist. Two men came with a strait-jacket.

Then somebody called the police canine corps. A trained dog-handler arrived with a leash and led the boxer away — to the lost-and-found department.

Birth of Pups Brings on Crash

WATKINS GLEN (AP)— A mother who just could not wait caused a pickup truck in which she was riding to crash into a utility pole Tuesday night, knocking out power in a rural area near here for more than an hour.

Thomas J. Coleman, 21, of Watkins Glen, told investigators he was returning home from the veterinarian with his pregnant dog when she jumped into his lap and proceeded to give birth to a litter of pups.

Dog Eats Preserved Heart and Alcohol Goes to Its Head

Snowball, a Spitz dog that belongs to Mr. and Mrs. Dale Huxman of Pretty Prairie, Kan., had an intoxicating experience after he ate some beef heart, The Salina Journal reports.

The Huxmans' daughter, Cheryl, was writing a science report on the subject of the heart. To give her report more meaning, she placed half a beef heart in a jar of alcohol. When she brought the display home from school, her mother threw it out.

Snowball took the heart, well-preserved by the alcohol, for a free meal and devoured it. Some time later, Mr. Huxman came in from the barn to ask his wife what was wrong with the dog.

"He acts crazy," Mr. Huxman said, explaining that Snowball was stumbling around inside the barn, bumping into everything and barely able to stay on his feet. They dog finally keeled over and slept it off.

Dog 'Registers a Vote'

LEXINGTON, Ky. (AP) — When Mrs. June Griffith filed a report on her expenses for running in a campaign for the state legislature, she listed as expenses $3 for a tetanus shot and $2.75 for a pair of hose. She explained that while campaigning she had been bitten by a dog.

Opera 'Goes to the Dogs'

HOUSTON, Tex. (AP) — Opera has literally gone to the dogs here. Some 40 dogs, from Great Danes to Chihuahuas, auditioned for 15 available parts in "Opera — Gone to the Dogs," one of the numbers of a local musical revue, "Showtime '72."

Dog's Diet
Is 'Rounded'

LIVERMORE, Calif. (AP) — When Mrs. Arlene Higuera's pet dog seemed to be getting more sluggish every day, she took the animal to a veterinarian. He operated and removed 267 marbles from the pooch's stomach. The pet recovered quickly.

Watchdog Fails
His First Duty

SOUTH SHIELDS, England (UPI) — Thieves who broke into the Douglas Vaults pub last week got away with cash, whisky, cigarettes and King, a Labrador dog doing his very first night of guard duty in the pub.

King turned up the next day and is back on the job. Pub owner Norman Deacon hopes he'll do better next time.

"He has started to bark at strangers," Deacon said.

Thieves Can Keep Car, Woman Wants Dog in It

CHICAGO (AP) — In an open message to thieves who stole her 1968 Cadillac, Mrs. Nancy Pindiak said, "Keep the car but return the dog."

The car was stolen from a shopping center in suburban Lombard.

"Our 12-year-old pet, Pepper, was in it and we'll give a $500 reward for his return," Mrs. Findiak said.

Pepper was wearing a gray tweed doggy coat with a black velvet collar.

"He has arthritis and needs special food," she said.

Dog Toilet Plan Studied

CAPETOWN, South Africa (AP)—The City Council is studying plans to install toilets for dogs, to prevent them from dirtying the streets.

MEETING WITH SKUNK 'SICKENS' POLICE DOG

ERIE, Pa. (UPI) — Inspector Sam Gemelli, Chief of the Erie Police Department's K-9 patrol division, was a little surprised when he found a report signed by "Duke," one of his dogs.

The note read:

"Sir:

"While in pursuit of a suspect at 4 A.M. this date I got on the wrong track and was powderpuffed by a Peppy Lepew, a local skunk of unknown address.

"After having a bath to no avail my snout doesn't work and I was wondering if this falls into the 'injured on duty' category. If so, please let me know — not necessarily in person—as I am very sick and not smelling very well."

Inspector Gemelli said Duke had said nothing in his report about his master, Patrolman Jim Perfetto, who got "skunked" along with Duke when the dog checked out some rustling bushes in pursuit of a prowler.

St. Bernard Dog Winds Up The Rescued, Not Rescuer

DEERFIELD, N.H. (AP) — Robert Gagnon and his son managed to rescue their 200-pound-plus St. Bernard, "Major," who had fallen through thin ice nearly 100 yards from shore in a pond.

Notified by a neighbor of the dog's plight, they rushed to the pond in a truck.

"We found a boat on shore, got two pieces of lumber and headed toward him," Mr. Gagnon said. "He was too heavy to get in the boat, so we pulled him to the truck. When we got him home, we rubbed him down and used my wife's hair dryer to dry him off."

Drinking Milk Makes A Dog Just Look 'Mad'

PENDLETON, Ore. (AP) — When the Umatilla County sheriff's office received several telephone calls about a big white dog that was foaming at the mouth, Deputy Russell Bartlett was armed with dog-catching equipment and sent to the rescue.

He caught the dog.

Then he found out that its owner had been feeding powdered milk to a batch of kittens. The greedy dog had been raiding the kitten's lunch and had come away with his muzzle covered with harmless white foam.

A Briton Is Fit to Be Tied After Her Dog Gets Loose

LONDON (AP)—Mrs. Jessie Way is seeking compensation from the Hammersmith district council because her pedigree boxer bitch, Tammy, was accidentally let out by municipal workmen and the result was eight mongrel pups.

"It's costing me around $24 a week," explained Mrs. Way. "I obviously can't sue the father for maintenance, but I think the council should pay up."

Washing Dog in Tub Turns Emergency

INDIANAPOLIS (AP) — "My sister was washing the dog in the bathtub and her toe got stuck in the drain," said the young female voice.

So, like any good dispatcher, Marty Smith of the Lawrence Volunteer Fire Department sent a rescue unit to the trailer home.

Firemen were surprised when they arrived and found the toe didn't belong to the caller's sister—it was a paw belonging to their female dog.

An assistant fire chief deftly freed the animal.

Just Too Young

TORONTO, Ont. (AP) — Don't expect a pup to do a big dog's job. A service station owner found that out when thieves broke into his station and stole the 3-month-old German shepherd standing guard.

BATHROOM FOR DOGS IS LIKE CHILD'S PLAY

NORTH STONINGTON, Conn. (UPI)—There is one drawback to Connecticut's new canine comfort station.

The sand-filled trench complete with fire hydrants sometimes is mistaken for a children's playground, officials say.

The station, at a rest area off Interstate 95, recently was opened by the state department of transportation. It may well be the nation's only facility.

The two fire hydrants include one colored soft pink and the other baby blue, despite the fact dogs are color blind.

To straighten out those who confuse the area with a children's playground, officials say they will post signs. The problem with that is the signs may confuse the dogs.

DRUM STICKS CHASE AN UNWELCOME DOG

ROCKFORD, Ill. (AP)—Ella Milner, 14 years old, tried everything to chase away a dog that followed her on her way home from school, but to no avail.

"He was a very friendly dog," Miss Milner said. "I took a look at his tags. I'm not making this up —his name really was Snoopy on one of the tags. He looked something like Snoopy, but shorter than a beagle.

"He kept following me, so finally I sat down, took out my drum sticks, and started drumming on my drum drill book. I played 'Go Tell Aunty Rhody' and he was a pretty good listener —for about five minutes.

"Then he got up and left. I didn't think my drumming was that bad."

FOOD FIREMEN LEFT 'GOES TO THE DOGS'

PUEBLO, Colo. (AP)—When firemen from Fire Station No. 5 put their supper on the table recently, the fire alarm sounded and they had to leave.

W. E. Lucas, a fireman, had left a porterhouse steak, Capt. Don Williams had abandoned his rib steak and Tony Herrera left behind his cold cuts.

When they returned, two sets of greasy puppy prints were evident on the table. The cold cuts and rib steak were intact, but the porterhouse was missing.

The firemen followed the puppy tracks but not a puppy or even a bone was found.

It was pointed out that the dogs were smart enough to take the choicest cut of meat.

'Barking Man' Is Fined

ROCHFORD, England (AP) — A man who barked back at a dog was fined $12. He admitted using insulting words and behavior toward the dog and its owner during a scuffle.

Kitten Uses Bottle as House

POINT PLACE, Ohio (AP)— Some people have model ships or flowers ensconced in glass bottles, but Jaimie Boyer has a kitten in a bottle. A live kitten. His young Siamese, Dingy, has developed an affinity for a glass bottle. She squeezes in and out when the bottle is placed horizontally.

Boy Trying to Help His Cat Gets Stuck in Tree Himself

RAVENNA, Ohio (AP) — "Alley Cat" went exploring one of the large trees in the backyard of his owner's home and got stuck.

Six-year-old Ricky Bates decided he would be his pet cat's hero and climbed up to save him.

"Alley Cat" got free and ran off, but Ricky got stuck.

The City Fire Department was called and Capt. Jake Oostdyk became Ricky's hero.

Dead End Street
To Save His Cat

FARNBOROUGH, England (UPI) — One after another, little Nicholas Dungay's three kittens died under the wheels of cars speeding past his home on Sycamore Road.

So Nicholas, 9, got up a neighborhood petition to the Farnborough Council to make the road safer.

The council declared it a dead end street.

Cat Saves Family
of Three

LINCOLN, Neb. Jan. 2 (AP) — A cat awakened one member of the Arnold Otto family today and all three family members fled from a fire that engulfed their two-story frame home. The cat died in the fire. "They would all have been killed if Mrs. Otto had not heard the cat," said Fire Chief Mel Keller.

CAT LEFT A FORTUNE LIVES IN HIGH STYLE

CHARLOTTE, N.C. (UPI)— Tommie, a fat cat in the truest sense, is living proof that felines, even rich ones, are finicky.

The cat, of unknown lineage and age, is the sole surviving beneficiary of a $200,000 estate left when his mistress, Mrs. Andree P. Montst, died in 1965.

Tommie has an entire house to himself and a full-time housekeeper to look after him.

But despite his fabulous wealth, neighbors report that Tommie is getting grumpy in his old age. Said 24-year-old Michael Summers, who lives nearby:

"I tried to pet it and it bit me. I was just trying to be friendly."

Tommie, rumored to weigh about 28 pounds, though his keeper won't comment, spends most of his days sunning himself on the porch of his residence at 2101 Hastings Drive.

After his death, his share of the estate will be divided between the Catholic Church and the Charlotte Rehabilitation Hospital.

39

Rider Makes Engine Purr

WINFARTHING, England (UPI) — Reginald Last said he lifted the hood of his car to check a strange sputtering noise Wednesday and found a large white cat perched on the top of the motor block.

"He must have traveled there for miles," Last said. "He was very dirty and a bit roughed up."

'Watchcat' in Florida Growls and Then Runs

MIAMI (AP) — Mrs. E. H. Stafford doesn't need a watchdog.

She prefers her watchcat.

The Siamese cat sits in a long, low window. If anyone approaches, he utters a horrible growl.

His "protection" ends here. After growling, the cat retreats under the bed.

SUIT OVER BEQUEST TO A CAT IS SETTLED

MUSKEGON, Mich., March 19 (UPI)—Angel is the fattest cat in Muskegon, maybe in all the world.

Her guardian, Mrs. Donna Plichta, has built Angel a 10-by-10-foot home, with a well for fresh water and an electric heater to ward off the night chill.

All this was made possible by a bequest of $63,000.

The bequest brought lawsuits that Muskegon County Circuit Judge James F. Schoener resolved yesterday.

Mr. Schoener approved a settlement that divided up a contested one-third of the estate of Helen Below, a former Muskegon policewoman who died in mid-1972. Miss Below left her entire estate of property, cash and stock shares to her cats, Angel and Satan.

The legal problems stemmed from a stipulation in the will that upon the deaths of Angel and Satan, the estate should go in equal shares to Mrs. Plichta, to her mother, and to the Muskegon County Humane Society.

The troubles arose when the society was dissolved and was succeeded by three other animal care organizations.

Cat Bells Voted in Florida

DEERFIELD BEACH, Fla., Feb. 9 (AP) — The City Commission has passed an ordinance requiring cats to wear bells. The commissioners adopted the motion after a local Audubon Society member protested that silent cats were decimating the bird population. Any owner who fails to tie a bell to his cats can be fined $25.

Firemen Wind Up Redfaced Trying to Aid Cat in a Tree

KANSAS CITY (AP) — Firemen had tried for two days to get a cat down from a tree—first with a ladder and then with water from a pumper truck. Nothing worked.

Then 21-year-old Richard McClain tried his hand.

"I climbed up the tree and just shook it loose," he said. "It was simple."

Pet Cat Given Crown of Gold

LOS ALTOS, Calif. (AP) — Dr. L. Barry Thielke's dental practice may expand if Shiramir refers his feline comrades.

Shiramir, also known as Oscar around the house, had a gold crown installed in his mouth this week by Thielke, the 2-year-old Persian cat's owner and a dentist.

And the 34-year-old Thielke says he may continue treating cats.

"Once such a feat is accomplished with a good prognosis, there's always the possibility of referrals," Thielke said.

He said he examined his cat's mouth one night and discovered a fracture involving half a tooth. Although he had never undertaken such a task before, Thielke decided that human and cat teeth arrangements were not that dissimilar.

2.

Flying High

2 Owls Drafted to Live In Smithsonian's Tower

WASHINGTON, Feb. 9 (AP)—The Smithsonian Institution has drafted two owls to occupy the deserted five-story tower on its castle.

They are being kept inside, behind locked windows, in the hope they will get used to the idea of making it their home.

For more than a century owls lived in the castle tower, but in the mid-nineteen-fifties they flew out one morning and the windows were locked when they returned.

Dr. Alexander Wetmore, who was secretary of the Smithsonian from 1934 to 1952, said, "The owls weren't tidy and the business people couldn't stand that, so one day they just sanitized everything."

About two years ago, in a policy change, the Smithsonian opened the windows, but no owls showed up.

The drafted owls, a male and a female, came from the National Zoo.

Swan Breaks With Tradition

RIO DE JANEIRO (AP) —A female swan has upset an old saying that when one swan dies, its mate expires from grief. When the swan's mate was killed in a duel with another male, she made advances to the winner.

PET PIGEON HITCHES RIDES ON FAMILY CAR

CORPUS CHRISTI, Tex. (AP)—When Mr. and Mrs. John Gold leave for work each morning, Gooney, their pet pigeon, clings to the car's windshield wiper and accompanies them part of the way.

When the Golds near their home on return from work in the evening, the pigeon flies out to meet them for a few blocks.

The bird also accompanies their daughter, Linda, to school each morning.

Gooney has been with the family ever since he was found injured and nursed back to health several months ago.

Music Doesn't
'Send' Birds

SAN FRANCISCO (AP) —
Harry Marcus believes he has
proof that birds love classical
music. Two different families of
birds have made their homes in
Mr. Marcus's two stereo speakers
in his backyard, and no matter
how loud Beethoven is blared,
they won't leave.

KO'd by goose to his 'hardest fall'

LOS ANGELES — Joey Bar-
num fought the best welterweight
of his day and lost only a handful
of his 250 pro and amateur bouts.

In the 40's and early 50's he
fought stirring battles with En-
rique Bolanos, Willie Joyce,
Aldo Spoldi, Bob Montgomery
and the Docusen boys, Maxie and
Bernie.

But on Friday, he was kayoed
by a goose.

"It was the hardest fall I ever
took," he said ruefully as he sat,
his trousers torn and his legs
bleeding, glaring at the Brown
Goose which chased him in a Los
Angeles park.

"I've never taken that much of
a beating in the ring," he said.

"Three of them came at me, and this one that was obviously the leader, you couldn't stop him."

Barnum, a bail bondsman, was walking through the small park towards a sheriff's office to post bail for a customer when he was attacked.

Deputy Carl Nelson said one of the geese has been nesting in the ivy near the building entrance, but thus far no one had complained about being attacked.

"I complained," snapped Barnum. "I said to one of those guys, 'If I'd thrown a right at one of those damned geese, and broken its neck, what would you have done then?'

"And you know what this guy said? He said: 'Well, I suppose we'd have buried it.' "

Bath Is Heated for Birds

CHATTANOOGA (AP) — After trying several years to find a way to keep water in her old bird bath from freezing during the winter, Mrs. Rose Bokina has solved the problem. She made it into a structure with a heating unit and thermostat. She hopes the warm bath will attract birds all year.

Ostriches Are 'Watchdogs'

PORT ELIZABETH, South Africa (AP)—A property owner here keeps two ostriches, which he says pounce on trespassers.

Woodpecker Is Culprit In Home 'Vandalism'

FOULSHAM, England (AP)—When cottage-owner Henry Reed complained to Norfolk police after mysterious holes appeared in the outer wall of his home, vandalism was discounted.

One of the investigating officers, a bird enthusiast, pinpointed the culprit immediately — the holes were caused by a woodpecker in search of insect larvae.

This Is One Party He Should've Ducked

SAN DIEGO, Calif. (UPI) — Clyde Meyer was fed up with hunting.

What with illness, and sitting around in bad weather enduring the discomforts of duck blinds, he decided he wanted no more of it. Meyer gave up the sport, sold his guns, and gave up his membership in a duck hunting club.

He agreed, as a favor to a friend, to attend the annual party of Ducks Unlimited. His condition was that he wouldn't have to do any hunting.

Meyer, it turned out today, won the gathering's door prize—an all expenses paid duck hunting trip.

A Peahen in Kansas Finds Lightbulb Just Won't Hatch

HUTCHINSON, Kan. (AP)— A peahen, owned by Mrs. C. H. Bailey of Hutchinson, sat patiently on her nest for 28 days, while a peacock strutted nervously nearby.

At last, the peahen deserted the nest, and Mrs. Bailey rushed to the nest expecting to see a downy peacock chick.

Instead, she found only a discarded lightbulb, which apparently had fooled the peahen for four weeks.

A PET CHICAGO DUCK THINKS HE IS A DOG

CHICAGO (AP) — Mr. Duck is more than a duck around the Bob Brophy home.

He has turned the tables on the family watchdog, Duffer, and guards the house from intruders.

The eight-pound web-footed bundle of white feathers had had no formal training in the art of home defending and thinks he is a dog.

A duck house was built in the backyard for Mr. Duck. When Mr. Duck took possession, Duffer moved in, too.

"I'm sure he thinks he is a dog," said Mrs. Brophy. "He quacks when strangers come into the yard and his quack is more like a bark than the sound other ducks make."

He's No Dumb Cluck In 'Emergency' Case

PROVO, Utah (UPI) — J. L. Gull is a bird who knows where to go when he is in a gooey mess.

While most other seagulls were asleep, J.L., oil-drenched and unable to fly, waddled into a hospital emergency ward before dawn Monday.

Surprised staff members gave the bird a bath, food, and registered their new patient as "J.L. Gull," a reference to Jonathan Livingston Seagull, the hero and title of a best-selling book.

"We saw the bird just waddling down the hallway all dark and greasy," said nurse Cheryl Giles, 26. "Our door is usually open and it just walked right in."

After being treated, J.L. posed for television cameras and was visited by veterinarians. They decided he was "cleansed sufficiently" to be put on the outpatient list.

The Utah Fish and Game Department released the seagull Monday night at Utah Lake, a large body of fresh water just west of Provo.

The seagull's condition set off an investigation of possible oil spills in the area. Utah Lake was found to be clean, but an oily scum was found at a U.S. Steel holding pond where a lot of seagulls congregate.

The seagull has been highly respected in Utah since 1847, when flocks of the birds saved the pioneer Mormon's crops by eating swarms of crickets that blackened the sky.

For the feat, the seagulls earned a gold monument, the title of state bird, and a place forever in Mormon history. Gulls now abound in the state.

In the book for whom J.L. Gull was named, Jonathan Livingston Seagull was a bird who dared to be different from the flock. While the rest fought for scraps of garbage from fishing boats, Jonathan was seeking freedom through the perfection of flight.

Buzzard Feathers Cause Trouble at Court in Florida

MIAMI (AP)—A few buzzards took a bath on the roof of the 25-story courthouse building and caused the malfunctioning of elevators in the building, said John McCue, assistant county manager.

"It's their molting season," he said of the birds that nested atop the courthouse.

"The heavy rains just washed a lot of their feathers into the drains, and they were clogged. The water was running into the windows on the top floors, and it short-circuited the elevators."

Speed Limit for Birds

FORT WAYNE, Ind. (AP) — Someone is apparently regulating the traffic of birds. A traffic sign reading "Speed limit 30" has appeared at the top of a tall evergreen tree here.

Someone Plays 'Shell Game' With a Hen's Egg in Maine

PITTSFIELD, Me. (AP) —John Curtis, a policeman, says he has no idea who planted the nest egg in his hen house. But he doesn't believe in hens laying golden eggs.

Mr. Curtis's daughter, Kathy, 10 years old, said that when she went out to collect the morning eggs she lifted a nesting hen and there it was—an egg wrapped in a five-dollar bill and tied with a blue ribbon.

2 Ducks Shot in California Set Off a 'Treasure Hunt'

TULELAKE, Calif. (UPI) —Two ducks with golden gizzards were found recently in this tiny Siskiyou County community near the Oregon border.

Mrs. John Thompson said she found flecks of gold in the gizzards of two red-head ducks shot during the hunting season.

Local duck hunters are on the scent of the ducks' migration route, hoping to find a new bonanza of gold.

The largest piece of the metal was a quarter-inch in diameter and was valued at about 50 cents.

Parrot Is Helping to Teach Mutes in Hospital to Talk

NEWARK, England (UPI)—A parrot is teaching mute patients to talk.

The nursing staff at the hospital near here put the parrot, named Peter, in a ward with 40 men suffering from a mental disability that prevents them from speaking properly.

Every day, for 18 months, Peter kept up a nonstop flow of words. Then one of the patients started to say simple words correctly.

Now the parrot is helping teach the other patients to talk. The nurses point to objects and Peter repeats the names over and over.

One Man's Goose, but His 'Guard'

PHOENIX, Ariz. (AP)— Henry Wimberg has won the right to let a Superior Court jury determine if he can keep "watchgeese" on his property. Maricopa County Superior Court Judge Howard Peterson ruled that Wimberg, 41, should have wide latitude including the jury trial to appeal his City Court conviction for keeping four geese in his undersized front yard.

Wimberg was convicted Dec. 21, 1971, of violating a city ordinance requiring 10,000 square feet to keep fowl and other animals except household pets. His front yard is 6,400 square feet.

"I testified under oath that they were my pets, used as watchdogs," he told Peterson. "Yet, I was convicted with no showing that they were a nuisance to anybody."

Kidnapped Spanish Eagle To Be Flown Back Home

SAN FRANCISCO, Oct. 23 (UPI)—A rare Spanish imperial eagle, mysteriously kidnapped from a bird preserve in Spain, will be returned to its home.

The 12-pound, two-foot high bird named Vie, one of only 100 of its species, was captured by state agents who were pursuing a car when the bird was released and flew from the car's window.

The two-year-old bird will be flown to its 5,000-acre home in Spain by commercial jet in the care of a bird specialist.

Policeman Says Bluejays Are Destroying His House

PORTLAND, Ore. (AP) — Larry Straub, a Portland policeman, says bluejays are destroying his house.

Mr. Straub, who has filbert trees in his yard, says jays grip nuts in their claws and beat on them with their beaks while balancing on his roofbeams. In so doing, they beat the shingles off his house. The last rain washed so many nuts off his roof, he said, that his drainpipes clogged.

Chickens Play For Their Lives

BUENA PARK, Calif. (UPI) — Chickens at Knott's Berry Farm are escaping the frying pan by keeping tourists entertained.

For 10 cents a tune, the trained chickens peck out a rough melody at a tiny keyboard. Their reward is a handful of chicken feed mix and an increased life expectancy. For the owners, it means up to $10 a day.

The chickens are trained for about an hour a day for seven to nine weeks. The average career of a feathered pianist is about five years. Joe Green a trainer's assistant at the amusement farm, notes that few roosters are ever used. "They have to take time out to strut around and crow," said Green. "Hens don't."

Robin Family Likes Home in Mohonasen Bus

Some birds live in a golden cage and some in a bus. A bus?

That's right, according to Mrs. Mary Palmatier, a bus driver for the Mohonasen Central School District, who told the Gazette a persistent family of robins has three times built its nest in the grill of Bus 29 which she drives.

Mrs. Palmatier removed the first two nests and placed them in a tree near the Mohonasen bus garage on Helderberg Avenue. Then, last weekend, the robins built a third, larger nest of mud and straw in the bus grill.

The nest is still there and the birds are living in it when the bus is parked at the garage. Their choice of a home does, however, present an occupancy problem.

When Mrs. Palmatier arrives for her first run in the morning, the robins vacate the nest for a tree. There they stay until the bus returns at the end of its run. Back into the nest they go . . . until the second run and the third of the day.

3.

Fish and Wildlife

12-Year-Old Texan Finds Fossil of 600-Pound Fish

GRAND PRAIRIE, Tex. (AP)—Twelve-year-old Gary Ford discovered the 100-million-year-old fossil of a 600-pound fish while digging for shark tooth fossils near his home.

Gary immediately notified the Dallas Museum of Natural History, and a museum crew moved in to do the excavation work.

"He's really a very well informed young man for his age," said the museum director, Hal Kirby. "Most people would have dug around and destroyed the fossil. He notified us first and had properly identified it as a fish even before we arrived."

A 'ONE-MAN PATROL' HUNTS COAST SKUNKS

LOS ANGELES (AP) — For six years now, Apolinar Ramos has been the one-man skunk patrol for the city's Department of Animal Regulation.

Mr. Ramos says he has trapped more than 5,000 skunks, while suffering only two "direct hits."

He says the skunk problem is getting worse.

"People keep moving into the hills where the skunks live," he explained, "and the skunks are afraid to move out because the coyotes will get them. Six years ago we got maybe 15 skunk calls a week. Now it's 20 to 30."

'Tern-About' Is Fair Play

BRIXHAM, England (UPI) — Members of a yacht club say they saw a fish kill a seagull.

They said when the bird dived recently to grab a fish in Brixham harbor, the fish grabbed the seagull, pulled it beneath the water, and drowned it.

6-Foot Texas Jackrabbit Is a Big Tourist Attraction

ODESSA, Tex. (UPI) — A six-foot-tall jackrabbit has become one of the major tourist attractions in the West Texas town of Odessa.

Many local residents thought it was a hare-brained idea when a travel director suggested the city build a monument to the area's number one resident. But the fiberglass replica of the long-eared beast has proved popular with visiting children since it was erected in 1962.

Raccoon Comes in from Cold

SHERBROOKE, Quebec, (Canadian Press) — A woman in this community, 77 miles southeast of Montreal, was awakened by a slight noise at the door — a raccoon. The animal came in when she opened the door, stayed for about 30 minutes to warm up, and left.

SKUNKS 'LOUSING UP' A WISCONSIN VILLAGE

WAUZEKA, Wis. (UPI) — Anyone who said this tiny Crawford County community of 494 residents smells would be correct.

It has been invaded by skunks.

"Nearly every yard in the village was dug up last summer by skunks in search of grub and cutworms," according to Dawald Craig, editor of The Kickapoo Papoose.

"And now the creatures have decided to stay through the winter," Mr. Craig said. "They're digging under the buildings and their unsavory odor permeates every corner of Wauzeka."

Mr. Craig said some skunks had been seen, more had been smelled, and "quite a few have been shot."

SHARKS 'DECORATED' IN SCIENTIFIC TESTS

WASHINGTON (AP) — If you meet a shark bearing bright red, yellow or blue decorations, tell the National Marine Fisheries Service laboratory in Narragansett, R.I.

About 10,000 sharks are now swimming the Atlantic Ocean bearing such tags, along with messages in five languages.

Three hundred and fifty of them have been recaptured as far away as 2,070 miles.

The investigations, which have been conducted for nine years, indicate so far that sharks travel a thousand miles or more annually, that the migratory routes of male, female and juvenile sharks of some species are different, and that some sharks may live much longer than supposed.

Pearl is Wedding 'Bonus'

INVERNESS, Scotland (AP)—A honeymooning couple received an unexpected wedding present when the bridegroom bit into a pearl buried in the flesh of a salmon.

Oregon Squirrel Stores Nuts for Long Winter

EUGENE, Ore. (UPI) — At least one squirrel in Oregon had prepared for a long, hard winter.

Rural firemen were called to inspect a clogged chimney and found it blocked by more than five pounds of filberts carefully arranged atop a brick ledge.

The firefighters investigated further and found the squirrel had also stashed another two pounds behind the eaves of the house.

TREES TOO HEALTHY TO 'SUIT' SQUIRRELS

PORTLAND, Ore. (AP) — The trouble with lush Laurelhurst Park on Portland's east side, from a squirrel's point of view, is that the trees are too healthy.

Charles Bruce, an Oregon State Game Commission ecologist, says the good condition of the trees means squirrels don't have any place to build their nests.

His solution to the problem of increasing the squirrel population of the park, which he estimates at five to seven eastern gray squirrels, is installation of houses.

"We tried this on the State Capitol grounds several years ago and now they have them coming out of their ears," he said.

Houses 10-by-20 inches have been built by students at MacLaren School for Boys in Woodburn for Mr. Bruce's project.

'FISH RAIN' REPORTED IN COAST COMMUNITY

OCEAN SHORES, Wash. (UPI) — "It rained cats and dogs," is an ancient hyperbole describing a heavy rainstorm.

But this real estate development on the Washington coast prefers to be more exotic.

It rained fish here recently.

Tom James reported that three or four dozen fingerling anchovies landed in his yard during the stormy winter day that poured 3.35 inches of rain on nearby Aberdeen.

Mr. James's chickens scrambled about eating the seafood delicacies that rained down from sky.

Harry Simpson, a State Fisheries Department official, said a water spout probably sucked the fish out of the ocean and they were blown half a mile inland by winds that gusted up to 50 knots.

Man's Skull and Shoes Are Found Inside Shark

ST. JOHN'S, Antigua (UPI) — The police reported that a 500-pound shark that had been caught had a man's skull and shoes in its stomach.

Bones and several empty tin cans were also found inside the nine-foot shark, which was caught by three fishermen near an offshore island, the police said.

The police were seeking to identify the skull, but said they had had no reports of missing persons in recent months.

Fish Is Caught 'Redhanded'

PERTH, Australia (AP)— A suburban housewife caught a freshwater red-clawed crayfish one morning with one of her home grown strawberries.

COMPANY SET TO USE MUSIC TO CHASE FISH

ERIE, Pa. (AP)—Most fish stories wind up with the fish getting off the hook, or even worse, on the platter. But the one told by Pennsylvania Electric Company has the fish swimming to the strains of popular music.

The company says it plans to drop speakers into the East and West Slip Bay waters of Lake Erie and pipe in contemporary music picked up from a local radio station.

Those who are supposed to know, the company says, assert that Gizzard Shad should make themselves scarce once the sounds of pop recording artists begin permeating the city waters.

The fish are drawn to the electric firm's water discharge pipes, which spill heated water from an electric facility.

The Gizzard Shad die from a lack of oxygen in the

warmed water, a company spokesman said, the result being a costly cleanup operation in the spring.

Rock music is needed, the spokesman said, because scientists say fish can become accustomed to music with a constant frequency.

Wrong-Way Moose Takes Lucky Turn

SAULT STE. MARIE, Mich. (AP)—Police in Sault Ste. Marie said a moose decided to swim across the St. Mary's River to Sault Ste. Marie, Ont., but he luckily didn't make it.

The moose set out from the American shore on Sunday but when he approached the Canadian side, picnickers scared him away and he swam instead to Sugar Island, back on the American side.

That gave him protection against the Ontario moose hunting season, which opened Monday.

British Fox Eludes Hounds With a 'Stop' at Local Pub

CLANFIELD, England (Canadian Press) — An Oxfordshire hunt was in full cry when the fox slipped the hounds by popping into the local pub. He scrambled onto the roof, down the chimney and out of a back window, much to the astonishment of huntsmen and drinkers.

"If ever a fox deserved to get away that one did," the landlord said.

This Woof No Wolf; Defects to Burglar

BALTIMORE (UPI) — John L. Weatherly, a South Baltimore garage owner, said he'll have to do some thinking before getting a new watchdog.

A burglar made off with $1,774 worth of tools early Tuesday and also took "Duke," Weatherly's nine-month-old German shepherd whom he was training to protect his garage.

"He was doing a pretty good job until yesterday," Weatherly said.

It's a Sign Town Fawns Over Deer

BUTLER, Ind. (AP) — Signs at the four main highways into this northern Indiana city read:

"Butler City Limits. Susie our pet deer lives here. Please drive carefully."

The 3-by-3-foot signs, with pictures of the deer, were purchased through donations from citizens and civic clubs in the town.

The pet deer has roamed the town since May 1971, when the community adopted her as a fawn after her mother was killed accidentally by construction workers at the edge of town.

She makes daily rounds begging handouts from housewives and the school children, often following them to school.

Racoon Makes 'Pig' of Itself

LIMA, Ill. (AP)—When Marvin Wilson, a farmer, looked over a litter of eight spotted pigs nursing on one of his sows, he discovered a new piggy associate: a baby raccoon.

4.

Down on the Farm

Western Union Is Told It Should Get a Horse

A latter-day version of the Pony Express can get through Manhattan's crowded streets a lot faster than a modern telegram, according to Assemblyman Stephen J. Solarz of Brooklyn.

Mr. Solarz, on Tuesday, told members of the Public Service Commission at a hearing into the quality of Western Union service that in a test two months ago he rented a horse and messenger and dispatched them across Manhattan. Simultaneously, he said, he handed in a telegram to a Western Union office.

The horse arrived hours ahead of the telegram, he said. Other witnesses at the hearings into the nation's privately owned telegram monopoly told of telegrams that arrived days late or never arrived at all.

A Pig in a Poke Hard on the Purse

TOKYO (AP) — A hog in Japan had a yen for yen, $377 worth to be exact. A hog trader laid the yen down while haggling with a prospective buyer and the hog ate the money, the Japan Times reported.

Rent-a-Cow Trend Producing Moola

RACINE, Wis. (AP) — Rent-a-cow agencies are flourishing in Wisconsin and may set a national trend. Wisconsin Agriculturist, a rural magazine, reports that rent-a-cow businesses are proving popular because of the rising price of dairy cows.

Today a good dairy cow costs about $600. You can rent one for $12.50 a month.

The magazine says that renting a cow is often better than owning one, particularly if the dairyman must go into debt in order to build or expand a herd.

Trees 'Catch' Horse

SANTA MARIA, Calif. (AP)—A horse got stuck between two trees while pasturing here and had to be rescued by firemen. They tied chains and ropes to the trees and bent them apart. The horse was unharmed.

Coeds Pay for College Babysitting with Pigs

CORVALLIS, Ore. (AP)—Debby Warren and Cynthia Harper are working their way through Oregon State University babysitting for some 1,250 pigs in the school's pig barns.

"It's been kind of hectic lately," Miss Warren said. "We've had to help at the birth of 150 pigs in one week. Sometimes we don't get a lot of sleep."

AN ARIZONAN OPENS MOTEL FOR HORSES

FLAGSTAFF, Ariz. (AP) — Tom Raptis isn't a cowboy, but his idea, he thinks, makes plain horse sense.

The Scottsdale businessman has opened the first of what he hopes will turn into a nationwide chain of motels for horses.

The first one, which accommodates 30 overnight guests, is a brown, steel barn four miles north of heavily traveled Interstate 40.

Mr. Raptis said he had been considering the idea since 1969.

"After noticing all the horses being trailered on the highways," he said, "I began wondering where their owners put them up for the night while the owners were sleeping comfortably in nice motel rooms."

After talking with several horsemen, Mr. Raptis says, he found out they had trouble finding accommodations for their four-legged companions.

He adds that the horse motel here is a pilot project. He charges $7 a night for each horse.

Pigs Like Pop Music

NEWMARKET, England (AP)—Robin Upton, a Suffolk pig farmer, finds pop music keeps his sows contented and helps them put on weight. "They listen to the radio most of the day," he said.

He Loses as His Horse Wins

RENTON, WASH. (UPI)—Dr. James Furuwaka had a sheepish look as he stood in the winner's circle beside his horse, Coco's Pal, at Longacres Race Track. The reason: He got mixed up at the betting window and put his money on someone else's horse.

Sounds Like a Lotta Bull in a Tight Place

ROME, Ga. (AP) — Now here's something you don't see every day—a 400-pound bull in the back of a car.

Floyd County police Sgt. Nedsel Acker and Patrolman Glenn Harper saw a four-door sedan moving slowly Thursday night and decided to investigate.

Acker and Harper said they found three men in the car, two of them sitting on the bull which was jammed between the front and back seats.

"How they got him [the bull] in there we don't know," the officers said. "Maybe they tranquilized him. He was just sitting there."

The men were lodged in the county jail on a charge of investigation, the officers said. The bull was lodged at an auto repair company.

"That's the only place we could find with a fence around it," the officers said.

License Plates on Horses?

KIEL, Germany (AP) — A provincial legislator proposed that horses have license tags affixed to their rear ends for identification in case of accident. The agriculture minister pleaded technical difficulties and said he had never heard of a hit-and-run horse anyway.

Bull Has No Right of Way

MILAN, Italy (AP) — An Italian court ruled that road-crossing animals never have the right of way, ordering Emilio Pellegatta to pay $1,666 in damages and court costs because his bull walked in front of an automobile, sending it into a ditch.

PIGS IN INDIANA GET 'ALL THE COMFORTS'

SHERIDAN, Ind. (AP)—Pigs live luxurious lives at Mr. and Mrs. David Rayl's pig farrowing barn.

The barn is not only air-conditioned but carpeted with more than 70 square yards of bright red material.

Mr. Rayl says carpeting serves a very useful purpose.

"Sometimes little pigs will get sore knees as they nurse," he said. "When that happens, they do not gain weight properly and there is always the possibility of infection and death."

All the refuse goes into a bin located beneath the farrowing floor, and when the gases from the refuse reach a certain level, a fan automatically turns on to ventilate the area.

There are also automatic feeders and watering fountains and the entire complex is lighted by fluorescent light.

Performing Steer Retires After 17 Years of Shows

AUBURN, Iowa (AP)—After 17 years in show business, George, a trained steer, is living a quiet life of retirement on an 80-acre farm near here with his owner-trainer, A.B. Patten.

During his years as a performer, George traveled 75,000 miles, to perform at county fairs and rodeos in 11 states.

"I'd ride ol' George out into the arena like a quarter horse," Mr. Patten said. "He'd cut a figure 8, make a square stop, back up, and kneel down for me to get off his back."

Among the steer's other tricks were rolling a barrel over a teeter-totter, crawling forward and backward on his knees, sitting up on his hind quarters like a dog and pawing the ground like a mad bull.

Goats Eat Keeper's Wallet

GALT, Ontario (AP) — A zoo keeper dropped his wallet while working in a pen with five goats. The goats ate $75 and a credit card before starting on the wallet.

Sheep Eats Heartily While Debate Rages

LONDON (AP) — A fully grown sheep found wandering near London's Euston Station has created a host of wooly problems for police. Frank Pawlowski claims ownership of the animal and says he wants to sacrifice it to a sun god in a religious ritual. The Society for Prevention of Cruelty to Animals says this is illegal.

While the dispute rages, the 3-year-old ewe has eaten all the roses around the police station where she is detained.

AN ARIZONA WOMAN FIGHTS FOR PET PIG

PHOENIX, Ariz. (UPI) — Mrs. Vincent Fusso and city authorities were having it out, and it was all over Burfie.

Burfie's problem is that he is a pig—and the Phoenix city code prohibits them.

"I am being summoned to court because of the drastic crime of having a pig," said Mrs. Fusso. "We can have a cow, we can have horses, we can have lambs, we can have goats, but we can't have a pig.

"The pig's only crime is that people think they smell, but pigs like Burfie don't smell if they are kept clean by people. It's the people, not the pigs, who are dirty."

Barring a change in the city code, Burfie must be gone when he reaches 200 pounds.

Patients at a Wales Hospital Do See Horses in the Halls

CARDIFF, Wales (UPI) — Patients at the Landsdown hospital can be forgiven for thinking they are delirious when they see horses galloping up and down the hospital corridors.

But the horses are real and frequently invade the hospital grounds, an issue of Medical News-Tribune reported.

In one case five amorous stallions chased their mares through the hospital buildings.

"We have no idea where they come from," a hospital spokesman said, "but they get in from time to time."

Farmer Calls Stolen Steers Out of 2,000 at a Feedlot

SELKIRK, Manitoba (AP)—Two steers stolen from Nick Reziniw, a farmer, were recovered by him a month later from a herd of 2,000 cattle at a feedlot 100 miles west of his farm when the animals recognized their owner's voice.

Mr. Reziniw traced his steers to an auction, then the feedlot.

He said the steers came forward "like babies" when he called their names.

5.

Scaly Scalawags

Crocodile Gets
Loose on Jet

PERTH, Australia (AP)— A 20-inch baby crocodile turned up on a passenger jet and ran down the aisle as stewardesses were serving coffee. A passenger trapped it in a blanket. The police said no one claimed owner- ship.

A New
Hampshire Girl
'Wears' Snake
on Neck

MANCHESTER, N.H. (AP) —Lu Gaudreault's household pet is a 6-foot-4-inch boa con- strictor named Alice. It was given to the 17-year-old high school senior by a friend as a birthday present.

Miss Gaudreault usually keeps the snake in a 20-gallon aquarium, but sometimes takes her for a walk.

"I was walking down the street with her," she said. "At first people thought I had a scarf around my neck and then they saw I had a snake and they really flipped out!"

2 SNAKES REAPPEAR OUT OF WOODWORK

COLUMBUS, Ga. (AP) — Eighteen months after Kerry Hand's pet boa constrictors, Boscow and Perifia, had escaped from a basket and crawled into the woodwork at his home, they were reunited.

Perifia, a 5-foot female, crawled back out and was recaptured six months after they disappeared.

However, there was no sign of Boscow, an 8-foot male, until a year later, when he stuck his head out of the same hole into which he had vanished, and was lured back.

"I was sure he had gone," said Kerry's mother, Martha Hand. "We don't know how he's been eating, but we used to have a problem with sewer rats where we live. They would come in from the outside sometimes. And we just realized that last winter we didn't have that kind of a problem."

CALIFORNIAN VISITED BY BOA CONSTRICTOR

HOLLYWOOD (UPI) — Here today and gone tomorrow, except that the poor rabbit forgot the law of the jungle and disappeared in record time.

The party responsible was a snake in the grass; but what a snake!

As William Hughes told the police, he was standing on the patio of his hillside home when he spied a rabbit squatting in the clearing below. Moments later a "huge" snake that closely resembled a boa constrictor gobbled the rabbit in one gulp.

Having taken his noonday meal, the engorged snake coiled itself around the trunk of a tree in Mr. Hughes's yard and displayed mild interest when the police flocked around. City animal control officers had been notified, but by the time they arrived, the snake got bored with publicity and slithered away.

Mr. Hughes was left to puzzle over the boa constrictor's new hunting ground.

Children of Ghana Village Play With Holy Crocodiles

ACCRA, Ghana (Reuters) —For the inhabitants of Paga, a small village on Ghana's northern border with Upper Volta, the crocodiles are their best friends.

For as long as people can remember the crocodile has been a sacred animal to the men of Paga, a symbol of their tribe, and it has been taboo to kill it.

The crocodile's special place has resulted in a rare phenomenon for this reptile which has been known on occasion to attack and eat men. The crocodiles of Paga play with the children. The game is called "Riding the Crocodile." It ends with a live chicken for the crocodile.

Snake Is Not in the Grass But Under a Power Mower

SPRINGFIELD, Mo. (AP) — Hugh Hough, 77 years old, was puzzled when his power mower wouldn't start.

He lifted the mower and looked underneath. Coiled around the underside was a 5-foot-8-inch boa constrictor.

The snake, believed to have belonged to a neighbor who had moved out, apparently made its home beneath the mower while the machine was in storage under a large tub.

Kansan Finds Alligator Wandering on His Lawn

WICHITA, Kan. (AP) — When Wayne McNabb stepped off his porch onto his front lawn on a recent morning, he was not "completely awake."

He woke up, however, when he noticed an 18-inch alligator snapping at him.

"I jumped like you wouldn't believe," said Mr. McNabb.

He and his wife had no idea where the animal had come from. They called the police and the alligator was taken to the Wichita Humane Society.

Gator's Authenticity Collegian's Relief

COLUMBIA, S.C. (AP)—A student walked into the University of South Carolina police station and said, "Look, I know you're going to think I'm drunk or something but I just saw an alligator crossing Green Street."

Campus police found a 4-foot gator swimming in a reflection pool in front of the campus library in downtown Columbia.

The reptile was turned over to wildlife officers who took it to the nearby Congaree Swamp. "He has a good home now and will be well taken care of," an officer said.

'Dead' Crocodile Revives

CAIRNS, Australia (Reuters) — Russell Yeullet, a camera technician, found a six-foot-long, apparently dead crocodile by the side of the road and threw it into his automobile. But the reptile had just been sunbathing, so Mr. Yeullet drove it, "snapping a bit," four miles to the Cairns Zoo.

Rock Singer's Snake Goes Down the Drain

NASHVILLE, Tenn. (AP) — Rock Singer Alice Cooper's pet boa constrictor, which vanished from his motel room last year, turned up dead in a drain pipe in the motel bar.

"Back in December we had a problem with the drains," motel manager Joe Ewing said, "and we just couldn't figure it out." Cooper reported leaving the snake in the bathroom of his room while he performed a concert.

Boa Bolts, Car Given Desnaking

BREMERTON, Wash. (UPI) —A four-foot boa constrictor named Dagon has proof positive that his owner, Cal Baines Jr., is fond of him.

Baines paid two automobile mechanics $14 per hour to dismantle his car to find Dagon.

Baines left Dagon in the car Saturday while he went shopping and returned just in time to see Dagon's tail disappearing up into the dashboard area by way of the clutch pedal.

Dagon was still hiding out Sunday, so Baines and a friend looked under the dashboard, under seats, and behind speakers but could find no boa constrictor.

Monday, Baines turned the job over to professionals, and mechanics Clarence Boschee and Earl Adams began their boa constrictor hunt.

They loosened the dashboard, pulled out heat hoses, took off the door panels, pulled out the back seat and removed practically everything that was removable on Baines' automobile.

There was no sign of Dagon.

After more than two hours of fruitless searching, the mechanics began pulling the fabric lining from the roof of the car and there was Dagon —all four feet of him stretched out on the middle of the frame above the windshield.

"We found him," said Boschee, "But somebody else can pull him out."

The frame had to be pried open, but Baines got his hand on the boa constrictor and coaxed it out of hiding.

"He's a little cold, but he's all right," said the delighted Baines.

Thief in Florida Steals Some Menacing Things

ST. PETERSBURG, Fla. (AP)—The police say there is a thief in St. Petersburg who might not have much taste, but, boy, does he have nerve.

Recently, officers said, someone heisted two alligators from a city-owned nature trail near Luke Maggiore. The gators — one 2-feet long and the other about 3 feet — were lifted from a pen.

Boa Constrictor Is Pet For an Oregon School

HILLSBORO, Ore. (AP) —Milhous spends the school day curled around a tree limb peering at students in Hillsboro Mid-High School.

Milhous is a 5-foot-long boa constrictor that lives in a display case in the school hallway.

"It doesn't take the kids long to notice him," said Franklyn Shinninger, a science teacher who takes care of the snake. "Before when we put things in the display case, the kids might glance at them. Now there is someone in front of the case all the time."

CHUMS SAVE HIS LIFE

NAIROBI, Kenya (AP)— A 10-year-old boy was grabbed by a crocodile, the official Kenyan News Agency reported, but escaped after seven schoolmates jumped on the beast and stuck their fingers in its eyes. The boy was later reported recovering satisfactorily in a hospital.

Baboons
and Zoos

Camel Escapes From Zoo And Hits Policeman In Head

ALAMOSA, Colo. (AP) — Tony the camel didn't bite the hand that fed him, but he did hit the officer in the head who tried to persuade him to return to the city zoo.

Tony somehow got out of the zoo and was heading for Adams State College Campus when he was intercepted.

Garland Parker, a policeman, received the blow in the head when he tried to stop the camel. Tony is back in the zoo and Mr. Parker is back on the job.

I'd walk a mile for a mild, mild Camel.

Saved Stamps

KNOXVILLE, Tenn. (AP) — Knoxville's zoo has two new black and white zebras — purchased with 2,500 books of trading stamps donated by local citizens.

Baboon's Flight Ends in Airport Ladies' Room

GLEN BURNIE, Md. (UPI)— An escaped 65-pound boy baboon led pursuers on a three-hour, slapstick chase through Friendship International Airport Wednesday but was finally nabbed when he ducked into the ladies' room.

The hairy, agile beast monkeyed around the airport complex, leaping over chairs and counters and running up and down long corridors. Frightened citizens scurried to shelter as police, state troopers and terminal employees charged the animal.

Officials said the baboon escaped from his cage in the airport freight area where he was awaiting delivery from New York to Johns Hopkins Hospital for a research project.

After showing off his razzle-dazzle running skills, the animal climbed through a window into the ladies' room where he was cornered. He was put to sleep with a shot from a tranquilizing gun and returned to his cage.

A spokesman for the airport police described the beast as "docile but very, very quick."

A Baboon in South Africa 'Takes Over' Phone System

CAPETOWN (AP) — Subscribers at Kloof Nek Forest were left to wonder about the new bug in the telephone system when bells rang for no reason and some heard only barks, growls and sucking sounds.

A baboon had gotten into the unattended exchange. It pulled instructions from the wall, pressed every button on the switchboard, spilt milk on the floor and finally ate the only pen of Michael Anhauser, the operator who had left for a few minutes.

"I don't know what to put in my report," Mr. Anhauser said.

BOAR INTRUDES

THOUARS, France (AP) — Members of the municipal council were deliberating serious business at the town hall when a wild boar charged into their midst. The 260-pound animal, which had outdistanced hunters in a nearby forest, was shot by a policeman.

Baboon Among Men Races Back to Zoo

MESQUITE, Tex. (AP) — A wayward baboon, who rode out of the World of Animals enclosure on top of a visitors' bus, took one look at the human race and apparently decided he preferred monkey business.

Leaping down at the parking lot, he scrambled over a 17-foot chain link fence, swam a moat and raced back among his own kind.

GROWLS IN THE NIGHT REPORTED TO POLICE

SYRACUSE (AP) — "You're going to think I'm nuts," a telephone caller told sheriff's deputies about 3:45 A.M. recently.

"But there is a bunch of lions and tigers growling outside my room. They're keeping me awake."

The caller was not crazy or having a bad dream.

Sheriff's deputies said a circus truck filled with eight lions and tigers were parked outside the Carrier Circle, Howard Johnson's Motel here.

The truck was en route to a circus, according to Deputy Joseph DiStaola.

"How do you tell eight growling felines to keep quiet?" Mr. DiStaola was asked.

"You don't," he replied.

Instead he told the animal trainer, who was staying overnight at the motel, to move the truck to a nearby gas station, where the animals would not disturb the guests.

A spokesman for the motel said she had no idea what cargo the guest was carrying in the truck when he checked in.

Elephant Eats Suitcase

CAIRO (AP) — Airport officials opened the freight compartment of an Indian jetliner and found a baby elephant munching on one of the suitcases, the Middle East News Agency reported. No one had remembered to feed him.

New Jersey Motorist Calls Police to Report Elephant

NORTH BRUNSWICK, N.J. (AP)—When a motorist phoned the police at 2 A.M. recently to report an elephant in a roadway, the police thought the caller "was crazy."

He wasn't.

When the police arrived at the scene, they found the elephant wandering around the intersection. The police said the elephant was the property of a circus that was in town.

While the animal stood by peacefully eating grass, the police got in touch with the circus, and it was led back to its tent.

Kangaroo Confuses Driver

CRAWLEY HILL, England (UPI) — Terry Smith told the police here that he had stopped his automobile at a red light when a kangaroo bounded across the front of the car. When the police asked Mr. Smith, 29, what he had for supper, he answered, "Just meat pie."

COMPUTER HELPING CHIMPANZEES TALK

ATLANTA (AP) — Lana, a chimpanzee at the Yerkes Regional Primate Research Center here, is learning to ''talk'' with the aid of a computer.

Scientists are trying to determine if apes can be taught to communicate by a visual technique.

Lana must put a bar above a keyboard and then punch out symbols.

She can punch out a sentence structure asking, ''Please, machine, give me a piece of banana.'' If the request is made correctly, it is granted; if an error is made, Lana must start again.

A Silver-Toothed Tiger

PHILADELPHIA (AP) — Kundar, a local zoo's 300-pound rare Siberian tiger, has had his teeth capped in silver. The tiger had broken the tips off his two lower canine teeth. They were infected and abscessing. So the zoo's dentist put the tiger under a general anesthetic and performed root-canal surgery.

Egyptian Cooks Say No To Monkey a la Zaire

CAIRO, March 5 (Agence France Presse) — Players of the Zaire national football team were asked to dine in their hotel rooms after a little gastronomic upset, the Middle East News Agency reported here.

It said Egyptian cooks at the Alexander hotel where the team was staying protested yesterday when they were presented with monkeys that had been brought from Zaire skinned and dressed.

The cooks refused to prepare what the Africans insisted was a national dish back home, and a lengthy discussion began.

Harmony was restored when the hotel management agreed to set aside part of the kitchens so that the players and their helpers could prepare their own meal.

7.

Small Fry

Frogs Fight in Malaysia

PENANG, Malaysia, March 26 (AP) — Two species of frogs battled for five hours today, an event that local residents believe portends a coming disaster but that zoologists say is a fight for breeding grounds. About 70 reportedly died in the battle.

British Girl Learns Things About the Rats and the Bees

MANCHESTER, England (AP) — Caroline Cook took three tame rats home as pets. Soon a few more "appeared."

Then 14-year-old Caroline had some 40 rats, and was advertising them for sale.

Her mother explained:

"A friend of Caroline's gave her three brown and white tame rats. Two turned out to be females and the other a male. But at the time we couldn't tell the difference.

"We know the difference now."

MONKEY WEARS OUT ITS WELCOME IN OHIO

AKRON, Ohio (AP)—The D. Bruce Mansfields could put up with a little monkeying around, but four days of it were getting a little ridiculous.

"It was a real shock when we first saw him," Mrs. Mansfield said of the monkey, who took up a temporary residence on their roof. "I threw him a banana and you could see this big grin on his face."

Just when Mrs. Mansfield was thinking what to do with the animal, the monkey this time went into the home of Mrs. J. C. Kime.

"He took the lids off everything in the kitchen. He even opened her (Mrs. Kime's) purse and took money out of it," Mrs. Kime's daughter said.

The monkey was finally lassoed and given away.

Motorists Periled By Swarming Bees

ELMIRA (AP)—Thousands of bees — some observers believed there were millions — swarmed across Route 17 outside Elmira Wednesday and created a nuisance to motorists and nearby householders.

State Police said a truck loaded with 8,000 pounds of bees and beehives broke down.

Troopers said the driver, Elwood Smith of Antwerp, N.Y., left the truck to get another one but wrote a note advising the bees would become restless if the temperature reached 65 degrees. The mercury climbed to 74 at midafternoon.

Police suggested that motorists close windows on their automobiles as they passed the scene.

Snails Race in British Pub

LEEDS, England (Canadian Press) — Snails went on a pub crawl when Don Harris organized a snail race in his Yorkshire tavern. The course: 12 inches along the pub's bar.

Virginia Woman Finds Pets Make 'Strange Bedfellows'

RICHMOND (AP) — Mrs. Charles Butler recently entered her son's room and found Horace, a white rat, and Snowball, a white cat, peacefully snoring on a bed.

They are part of the Butler family menagerie that includes chickens, a dog, fish, hamsters, and mice.

Although Snowball has an appetite for mice, "It really likes the white rat," Mrs. Butler said.

Worm Who Lived in a Shoe

NOVATA, Calif. (AP) — For some time Mrs. Eleanor Keeg noticed that her shoes, which had been made in Taiwan, had an odd sound when she walked. Finally, the heel on one shoe disintegrated. It exposed a worm, which apparently had been living within, hollowing out the inside of the heel.

New Zealand Tree Puts Bees on 'Trip'

WELLINGTON (AP) — New Zealand's golden-flowered kowhai tree is being blamed for sending thousands of bees on a drug "trip."

The bees were found in an apparent coma on the banks of the Mokihinui River.

Officials of the Agriculture and Fisheries Department say the kowhai has a narcotic effect on bees, which can suffer hallucinations after sipping the nectar. The bees usually recover.

Don't Hit the Lamb

GISBORNE, New Zealand (AP) — The Rakauroa Country Golf Club, near this sheep ranching and tourist center, has introduced a new fairway rule: "A ball must be moved at least three club lengths from a newborn lamb."

Death-Scented Ant Taken to Trash Heap

BOSTON — When ants recognize the scent given off by a dead ant, they carry its body out of the nest and deposit it with other refuse.

In a test, the chemical was daubed on a live ant, and other members of the colony repeatedly dragged the struggling insect onto the trash heap. Only after the aroma wore off was the ant able to enter the nest.

British Church Organ Becomes 'Quiet as Mice'

EMPSHOTT, England (UPI) — The local Anglican church's organ has been silenced by mice gnawing at its insides.

"We are faced with the possibility of replacing the organ," said Rev. John Russell, the vicar. "But not only is the church as quiet as a mouse, it is as poor as a churchmouse."

Girl Opens 'Hotel' for Pets Left by Vacationing Owners

HOLYROOD, Kan. (AP)— Patti Hokr, 13 years old, has opened a "hotel" for pets whose owners leave on vacations.

The hotel is in her backyard, and daily rates start at 35 cents.

"Most of the animals have been real good," Patti said.

"They're always glad to have their owners come home, but they look like they enjoy it here too."

She maintains yard-meal service twice daily and plays with her guests often.

Mouse is Cause For Alarm

MANCHESTER, England (AP) — The electronic burglar alarm at a Manchester club kept going off but nothing was ever stolen. A well-placed mousetrap finally collared the culprit, which had been scampering through the alarm's control beam.

Hamster Gets Into a Safe And Chews Up Currency

LINCOLN, Ill. (AP) — Tom Kerrick, pet shop operator, got a start when he opened the safe and found a hamster staring up at him.

After escaping its pen, it had secreted itself in the open safe.

The animal chewed up $60 in currency as well as two checks. Luckily, enough of them were intact so that they could be redeemed.

African Frogs Stir Warning

SAN DIEGO, Jan. 9 (UPI) — Fierce frogs brought from Africa for use in pregnancy tests are becoming a threat to the balance of nature. The African clawed frogs devour native American frogs, according to scientists at the San Diego Natural History Museum. The 5-inch long invaders now abound in a six-mile stretch of the Sweetwater and Mt. Helix River drainages, where they have replaced the domestic species, the scientists said.